HeLP!
I'm Allergic to
Everything

Over 50 Simple & Delicious Recipes
Free From The Top 10 Priority
Food Allergens

LORI DZIUBA

Tellwell Talent
www.tellwell.ca

ISBN
978-0-2288-5425-8 (Hardcover)
978-0-2288-5423-4 (Paperback)
978-0-2288-5424-1 (eBook)

Table of Contents

Acknowledgements

I'd like to say a great big thank you to a number of people:

- To Clare Cyr for your exceptional attention to detail.

- To Liz Agudelo of Agudelo Media for your creativity and acuity in managing my social media.

- To my family and friends for all of your support and input.

- Most of all to my husband and son for putting up with me during this journey, and for their honest, valued feedback as my cherished taste-testers.

Introduction

Food allergies and sensitivities have always been a familiar part of my life. My grandfather was allergic to seafood, my mom has celiac disease, my dad has oral allergy syndrome and I grew up lactose intolerant. Avoiding certain foods, managing cross-contamination and reading food labels was normal in my family.

When I was pregnant with my first (and only) child, I suddenly was no longer intolerant to lactose. I found out when I had accidentally ingested something that contained milk, and had no issues at all. Curious and craving milk desperately, I tried small amounts of various dairy products over a period of time. None of the foods caused me any symptoms whatsoever. Yes!! I could eat cheese and drink all the milk I wanted! I was thrilled to enjoy foods I was never able to before, and my pregnant body got the calcium it needed for my developing baby.

The freedom that came from no longer being lactose intolerant lasted throughout my pregnancy and for about two years afterward. Gradually I started to notice familiar, terrible gastrointestinal symptoms when I consumed any dairy. The symptoms became severe once again, so I stopped consuming dairy once again. That seemed to eliminate the issues. I was disappointed, but easily fell back into old patterns of label reading and avoidance. Life moved on.

My life was pretty amazing at this stage. My husband, son and I had recently moved from Ontario to a small town in Alberta, right next to Jasper National Park. This is one of the most beautiful places on Earth. People travel from all over the globe to visit the areas that we frequented with short road trips. My son, William, was a very active preschooler. Running and climbing were two of his favourite things. He had the energy and stamina to accompany us on many hikes. Of course, he didn't have the awareness required to keep his safety in mind. My husband, Rupert, bought them proper sized rock climbing harnesses, clamps and rope. Rupert tethered William to himself via the harnesses, clamps and a length of rope. We didn't mountain climb, but many of the trails were on the sides of mountains. If William in his exuberance happened to fall, he'd have to pull Rupert down with him, hence he was safe to explore. Our summer weekends were filled with day trips to actively explore all this beautiful area had to offer. We'd pack lunch and snacks, and off we'd go. Being active and outside in nature was such a gift.

Over time I started feeling sick more often than not. I would have such pain, bloating and other gastrointestinal issues. I also began to feel overwhelming lethargy. At first I just chalked it up to fatigue from raising such an active boy. But it soon became apparent to be much more and drastically affected my active lifestyle. I was diligent with avoiding dairy, but that didn't seem to be enough. It seemed like anytime I ate, I would be sick.

Considering my family history, I began an elimination diet trying to find answers, to no avail. I also sought medical help. My doctor sent me for many blood tests, an endoscopy and a colonoscopy. All tests came back negative. I was told I had irritable bowel syndrome (IBS) which is a label put on any undefinable gastrointestinal issue. On one hand I was relieved that I didn't have a serious medical issue, on the other hand very frustrated with no real answers to why I was so sick and tired all the time.

I began to research in earnest, as I was not willing to settle for feeling so unwell most of the time. I wanted my life back. Technically speaking, a food allergy involves an immune system response whereas an intolerance or sensitivity to food involves only the digestive system. A food allergy reaction will occur immediately; food intolerance will have a delayed reaction for several hours or up to several days. This delayed response is what makes identifying the foods responsible for symptoms so difficult.

During my research I learned of blood tests available to screen for food intolerances. The medical community continues to debate the accuracy and reliability of such tests, yet only has means of identifying food allergies. In desperate need of answers, I decided to have my blood screened for food intolerances.

When I received my results I was shocked at the number of foods I had an intolerance to, yet so relieved to finally have answers. I began making the necessary changes to my diet and the results were astonishing. It took time for my body to rid itself of foods that I was intolerant to, yet slowly my gastrointestinal issues cleared up, my pain and lethargy disappeared, my energy came back. I was gaining my life back.

I learned something very important when communicating to others about my food restrictions. Technically I have food intolerances not food allergies, yet to be taken seriously regarding my need to avoid certain foods I have developed the habit of stating "allergy" and not "intolerance". Most of us are not in the medical field and for the sake of simplicity I will continue to make reference to food allergies, even though I am addressing food intolerances.

Learning to live with multiple food allergies can be a very overwhelming experience, especially if developed as an adult. It takes a lot of time and energy to learn new ways to manage all aspects related to food. As adults we have well established likes and dislikes, ways we cook and bake and favourite items we purchase at the grocery store. We have to let go of old habits and learn so many new things.

I am here to make the learning journey easier for you. I want to impart helpful advice for things that I learned the hard way. I want to provide exceptional recipes, that are simple to make and delicious for everyone. You will find that and more in "Help! I am Allergic to Everything". I chose this title as that was my exact feeling when I learned about all the foods I needed to avoid.

I have to avoid all Top 10 priority allergens. Wheat, dairy, egg, peanut, tree nut, sesame, soy, fish, shellfish, and mustard are known as the priority allergens or the top ten food allergens.

When I began my new food allergy journey I had such a hard time finding recipes that I could use. Finding gluten free recipes? No problem. Find diary free recipes? No problem. Finding both gluten and dairy free recipes? Again, no problem. Trying to find recipes that also are egg free...hmmm... vegan recipes should be helpful. Except vegan recipes often contain various nuts, so those are not as helpful either. It quickly became apparent that unless I wanted to eat only salad for the rest of my life, I had to learn to make my own recipes.

This cookbook is filled with recipes that are simple to make, safe from **all** the priority allergens and delicious to eat. I have provided a variety of recipes for breakfast, lunch, supper and snacks. You will also find options to make changes within some of the recipes for variety.

You have to give up certain things when you have multiple food allergies, yet the enjoyment of delicious foods shouldn't be one of them. Food is meant to be enjoyed. So flip open the book, and begin to enjoy eating once again.

Lori

Sanity Savers

SUBSTITUTIONS

I wanted to supply a list of ingredients that can be used to replace the priority allergens. There are many options that can work for each of the Top 10 food allergens. Yet when you need to replace all ten items, it gets a lot more complicated.

You can substitute one or two ingredients successfully using information available about alternatives. However, knowing how each ingredient interacts and affects other ingredients is critical. Trying to use commonly known substitutes for multiple items within your regular recipes can result in disaster. I speak from experience. I have flushed many recipe attempts down the toilet trying to make regular recipes work. It has taken me years of research and experimenting to reach the level of comfort I now have in the kitchen.

So, instead of providing a list of substitutions that may or may not work, you will find tested recipes that are simple to make, safe from all of the priority food allergens, delicious to eat – with no substitutions required.

A NOTE ABOUT GLUTEN FREE FLOURS

There are many varieties of gluten free flours available today. Most gluten free flours have to be mixed in combination with starches to achieve favourable results. I cannot provide a formula for using different gluten free flours as there are far too many options. I have, however provided my own preferred All Purpose Gluten Free Flour Mix. I use this mix in all my baking recipes, as I have found it is what works best for me.

There are also many ready-made gluten free flour mixes available at stores. Each will contain different varieties of flours and starches so will yield different results when baking. Some gluten free flour mixes use beans or legumes to make the flour. This can be great, unless, like me you are also allergic to beans and legumes. Be sure to read all labels carefully, always.

When baking with gluten free flour, guar gum or xanthan gum often needs to be added to replicate the properties of gluten. It is important to know if your ready-made mix contains gum. If it does, there usually is no need to add more within a recipe. If no gum is included in the ready-made mix, a recipe should indicate how much gum is needed.

I do not add gum directly to my All Purpose Gluten Free Flour Mix. Each of my recipes will clearly indicate when and how much is required for best results.

A NOTE ABOUT OATS

Technically speaking, oats are gluten free. However, oats are often contaminated with gluten because they may be processed in the same facilities as gluten-containing grains like wheat, rye, and barley. It is strongly recommended that people who have a gluten intolerance and especially people with Celiac disease only consume oats that are certified to be gluten free.

USING STARCHES

Starches are commonly used as a thickener when cooking gluten free. I most often use cornstarch, but potato starch or arrowroot flour are equally effective. Choose whichever best suits your allergy needs. To thicken sauces or gravies, do not add starch directly, or it will become very lumpy. Instead, make a slurry with equal parts starch and cold water. Cold water works best when mixing with a starch. When a starch slurry is added to a sauce or gravy, thickening will occur once it is heated throughout.

WORKING WITH GLUTEN FREE DOUGH

The best trick I learned when handling gluten free dough is to work with wet hands. This keeps the dough from sticking to your hands. Keep a bowl of water on the counter as you work with the dough, wetting your hands repeatedly as required. Any excess water on the dough simply helps the dough become light and flaky. This is especially helpful when working with oat flour. I will even smooth oat flour dough with my fingertips using very wet hands. Lightly oiling my hands only lead to a greasy mess. Water was the key to success.

MEAL PLANNING AND FOOD PREPARATION

Planning ahead and food preparation are vital necessities when dealing with multiple food allergies. Being hungry and having nothing safe to eat on hand is a very frustrating experience.

However, there are simple solutions to help make things easier. Here are my most valued habits that I practice:

- If you are like me with only one person in the family with food allergies, save any supper leftovers in a small tupperware container. Place the container in the freezer. If you do this regularly, you will have a variety of single serve meals that only need to be warmed up. If you have no time to cook one day (or don't feel like it!) the allergic person can have a delicious, safe home cooked meal without the effort. Other family members with no food restrictions can make do with anything.

- Keep a variety of snack foods in the freezer – always.

  - My Energy Bites can be made in many varieties, freeze well and make excellent quick snacks. I even enjoy how they taste when frozen!
  - When you make muffins, put some in the freezer to grab for breakfast or a snack. Try my Morning Glory Muffins or Banana Chocolate Chip Muffins.
  - You can make my Applesauce Snack Cake, let it cool and cut into squares. Wrap each piece in plastic wrap, and then place all wrapped pieces in a Ziploc bag in the freezer.

- Keep your pantry stocked with safe snacks and don't let other family members eat them. They have many other options available to eat.

  - My Crunchy Snack Mix is so simple to make and stores well in the pantry. Make up a double batch and place in large tupperware containers or Ziploc bags. Or, store in several single serve containers that you can easily grab on your way out the door.
  - My Honey Roasted Granola is another super easy recipe. Make up a batch and store it in an airtight container in the pantry. Add it to dairy free yogurt and fruit, have a bowl with your dairy free milk of choice or snack on it plain.
  - Mix up the dry ingredients of my Ultimate Pancakes and store in an airtight container in the pantry. When you want to make just a few pancakes, add liquid ingredients and a portion of the dry mix in a small bowl and proceed.
  - Keep a variety of single serve fruit cups on hand to easily make different flavours of Overnight Oats.

This book gives you sanity saving skills and delicious recipes to help take away overwhelming feelings that come from living with multiple food allergies.

All Purpose Gluten Free Flour Mix

This is a pantry must-have. There are many gluten free flours on the market now, yet this mix continues to be my go-to flour for a number of reasons:

1. It works. It is versatile, hence the name "all purpose".
2. The ingredients are fairly common and readily available.
3. The combination is easily digestible.

It is essential to thoroughly whisk the mixture to ensure that a complete blend of ingredients is used each and every time you bake. I like to mix up a double batch so that I always have some ready to use when the baking mood strikes.

When baking with gluten free flour, guar gum or xanthan gum often needs to be added to replicate the properties of gluten. I do not add gum directly to my All Purpose Gluten Free Flour Mix. Each of my recipes will clearly indicate when and how much is required for best results.

INGREDIENTS
2 cups brown rice flour
1 cup white rice flour
¾ cup potato starch (**not** potato flour)
¾ cup tapioca starch

INSTRUCTIONS
1. Measure flours and starches into a large container or bowl.
2. Whisk all ingredients together until thoroughly combined.
3. Store in airtight container.

Breakfast Foods

Ultimate Pancakes

I call these my lifesaving pancakes. You can use the batter as is for a basic pancake, or add fruit and sugar to make a sweeter pancake. You can even add spices and flavours for a savoury pancake.

Something important to note is that these pancakes take longer to cook than regular wheat pancakes. Also, they do not bubble on the surface which is usually the sign that a pancake is ready to be flipped. Instead, wait until the bottom of the pancake is mostly firm before flipping and cooking the other side.

DRY INGREDIENTS
1 cup Gluten Free Flour Mix
¾ cup brown rice flour
1 ½ teaspoons baking powder
¼ teaspoon baking soda
¼ teaspoon guar gum powder

WET INGREDIENTS
1 ¾ - 2 cups dairy free milk of choice
1 teaspoon apple cider vinegar

INSTRUCTIONS
1. In a small bowl, add apple cider vinegar to milk, set aside.
2. Add all dry ingredients to a large mixing bowl, whisk together thoroughly.
3. Add milk and stir until combined. Batter should be pourable, yet not too thin; add more milk if necessary.
4. Heat a large non-stick skillet. Once hot, pour batter in desired sized pancakes.
5. Once the bottoms of pancakes are mostly firm, flip and cook the rest of the way through.
6. Repeat until mixture is used up.

Honey Roasted Granola

Simple. Simple. Simple. This granola has only four ingredients and minimal preparation. It has to bake slowly at a low temperature, which is the only time consuming part. It takes about an hour to bake in a 250° F oven, yet takes hardly any effort to prepare. Oats and shredded coconut get tossed in melted honey and coconut oil. The mixture is then spread out onto two baking trays before placing into the oven. Once the granola is cooled, store in airtight containers or large Ziploc bags.

INGREDIENTS

3 cups gluten free oats
1 cup shredded, unsweetened coconut
⅓ cup honey
⅓ cup coconut oil

INSTRUCTIONS

1. Preheat oven to 250° F.
2. Line two baking sheets with parchment paper.
3. In a large bowl add oats and shredded coconut, stir to combine, set aside.
4. In a separate, small, microwave safe bowl, add coconut oil and honey. Heat until melted - only about 30 seconds. Whisk to combine.
5. Pour liquid mixture over the oats and shredded coconut. Toss until well coated.
6. Spread granola mixture evenly onto prepared baking sheets.
7. Place in oven for 50- 60 minutes. Granola is done when golden brown.

Overnight Oats

Overnight Oats are the solution for rushed mornings. The basic recipe for overnight oats is simply a 1:1 ratio of oats and liquid stirred together. The mixture is put into an airtight container and left in the fridge overnight. In the morning, the mixture has turned soft and is ready to eat. No cooking is required.

Overnight Oats can be kept in the refrigerator, in airtight containers, for up to a week. So, prepare a variety of jars on Sunday and breakfasts for the week are done. Grab a jar and a spoon on your way out the door, and eat it at your desk. You can eat them directly from the jar.

The flavour combinations are as endless as your imagination. Milk of choice, water, fruit juice or any combination can be used for the liquid. Diced or pureed fruits of any kind can be added for some awesome flavour and nutrition. Honey or maple syrup can be added for sweetness. I like to use fruit cups in my overnight oats. They come in a variety of flavours, and are just the right size.

BASIC RECIPE INGREDIENTS:
½ cup gluten-free oats
½ cup milk of choice

INSTRUCTIONS
1. Mix all ingredients together.
2. Place into an airtight container.
3. Store in refrigerator overnight.
4. Oats are ready to eat the next day.

BANANA OVERNIGHT OATS
½ cup gluten-free oats
½ cup dairy free milk of choice
1 small banana diced
1 tablespoon honey

RASPBERRY OVERNIGHT OATS
½ cup gluten-free oats
½ cup dairy free yogurt
½ cup frozen raspberries, thawed
    (include melted juice too)

FRUIT CUP OVERNIGHT OATS
½ cup gluten-free oats
1 single serve fruit cup, fruit & juice
¼ cup dairy free milk of choice (or water)
1 tablespoon honey

APPLE CINNAMON OVERNIGHT OATS
½ cup gluten-free oats
1 peeled and diced apple
½ cup applesauce
¼ cup water
¼ teaspoon cinnamon

Snack Foods

Snack Crackers

The process of making crackers is actually fairly simple, especially if you follow my little tips and tricks. The first trick when working with gluten-free dough is to keep your hands wet. As you knead and mix the dough this will help prevent the dough from sticking to your hands. The other important tip is to roll the dough out between two pieces of parchment paper. This will serve a few purposes. The bottom sheet of parchment keeps the dough from sticking to your counter and can then easily be transferred to a baking sheet. The top sheet of parchment keeps the dough from sticking to your rolling pin as you flatten the dough.

Vegan margarine is used in these recipes. There are many varieties of vegan margarine available. Be sure to choose one that is safe for your allergies.

SWEET POTATO CRACKERS
DRY INGREDIENTS
2 cups Gluten Free Flour Mix
½ teaspoon guar gum
2½ teaspoons baking powder
¼ teaspoon salt

WET INGREDIENTS
¼ cup vegan margarine (melted)
1 cup sweet potato puree

OAT FLOUR CRACKERS
DRY INGREDIENTS
1 cup Gluten Free Flour Mix
1 cup gluten free oat flour
½ teaspoon guar gum
2½ teaspoons baking powder
¼ teaspoon salt

WET INGREDIENTS
¼ cup vegan margarine (melted)
¼ cup water
2 teaspoons honey (melted)

INSTRUCTIONS
1. Preheat oven to 400° F
2. Add all dry ingredients to a large mixing bowl, whisk to combine.
3. Add wet ingredients to dry ingredients.
4. Combine mixture until a play-dough like texture is reached; using your hands can be most effective.
5. Handle half the amount of dough at a time.
6. Using a rolling pin, roll dough out to ⅛ inch thickness between two pieces of parchment paper - ensure edges aren't thinner than the rest of the dough.
7. Transfer parchment to baking tray, removing top layer of parchment.
8. Repeat with other half of the dough.
9. Score dough with a knife or pizza cutter into bite sized pieces, or with small cookie cutters if desired.
10. Bake for 12-15 minutes. The crackers will be firm to the touch when done.
11. Once cooled, the crackers can be broken along the scored lines.
12. Store in a Ziploc bag or airtight container.

Crunchy Snack Mix

This mix is similar to Bits & Bites, yet has only safe ingredients. This recipe makes a large quantity and can conveniently be kept in your pantry. Store some in snack sized containers, and the remainder in a large Ziploc bag. This way you can just grab a container or two and go. Take it on road trips, hiking, to work or school.

This mix uses store-bought, gluten–free pretzels and cereals, and vegan margarine. Be sure to read ingredients on products each and every time you buy them. Companies have been known to change ingredients, yet not the packaging. Always ensure the ingredients are safe for your needs.

INGREDIENTS

2 cups Cheerios cereal
2 cups Rice Chex cereal
2 cups Crispix cereal
1 cup gluten free pretzels
½ cup vegan margarine
2 tablespoons Worcestershire sauce*
½ teaspoon garlic powder
¼ teaspoon onion powder

INSTRUCTIONS

1. Preheat oven to 250° F.
2. Line 2 baking trays with parchment paper.
3. Combine cereals and pretzels into an extra-large bowl, set aside.
4. Measure margarine into a microwave safe bowl and heat until melted.
5. Add Worcestershire Sauce and seasonings to melted margarine and whisk to combine.
6. Pour liquid mixture over cereal mixture and toss until thoroughly coated.
7. Spread snack mix evenly between the 2 prepared trays.
8. Bake 50-60 minutes.

Be sure to carefully read ingredients. Not all Worcestershire sauces are gluten free.

No Bake Energy Bites

With multiple food allergies, pre-packaged snack foods are a thing of the past. Yet, I still wanted something that was nutritious, tasty and portable. Energy Bites are the perfect solution. They are quick to make, can be made into a variety of flavours, and they freeze well. So, when you are going on a road trip, need snacks for school or work, just grab a few from the freezer, pop them into a container and head out.

The steps to making any flavour of No Bake Energy Bites are the same. The only trick to it is to achieve the right combination of dry and wet ingredients so the mixture can hold together well when rolling into small balls.

PINA COLADA ENERGY BITES
INGREDIENTS
2 cups gluten free quick oats
¾ cup unsweetened shredded coconut
1 cup crushed pineapple
¼ cup honey

CHOCOLATE CHIP ENERGY BITES
INGREDIENTS
2 cups gluten free quick oats
¾ cup unsweetened shredded coconut
½ cup date paste *(see below)*
¼ cup water
½ cup allergy safe chocolate chips

DATE PASTE
1. Add 2 cups of dates to a blender, cover with boiling water
2. Let sit for *at least* 10 minutes to soften dates.
3. Drain about half of the water into a container, set water aside.
4. Blend dates, adding more of the drained water until desired texture is reached.

INSTRUCTIONS
1. Line a baking tray with parchment paper.
2. Add all ingredients into a large mixing bowl and stir to combine.
3. Mixture should be able to hold together well when rolling into small balls.
4. Roll into small balls, and place on the prepared tray. *(The Energy Bites are ready to eat as is, yet I find it best to freeze them right away for convenience.)*
5. Place the tray directly into the freezer.
6. Once the Energy Bites are frozen, transfer them to a large Ziploc bag and store in the freezer.

Applesauce Snack Cake

This cake is filled with applesauce and an aromatic blend of spices. Your house will smell amazing as this bakes. Two full cups of applesauce make it a wholesome cake to have for a snack.

Once cooled, slice cake and wrap individual pieces in plastic wrap. Place wrapped pieces in the freezer in a Ziploc bag so you have quick grab and go treats on hand.

INGREDIENTS

2 cups unsweetened applesauce
½ cup coconut oil (melted)
½ cup brown sugar
2 cups Gluten Free Flour Mix
½ teaspoon guar gum
1 ½ teaspoons baking soda
1 teaspoon cinnamon
½ teaspoon nutmeg
¼ teaspoon ground cloves

INSTRUCTIONS

1. Preheat oven to 350° F. Lightly grease a 9x13 cake pan with coconut oil.
2. Add applesauce, melted coconut oil and sugar to a bowl, stir to combine.
3. In a separate bowl, add remaining ingredients, whisk to thoroughly combine.
4. Add wet mixture to dry mixture, stirring until just incorporated.
5. Pour batter into prepared pan. Bake for 25-35 minutes.
6. When done centre will be soft, but not runny.

Cake batter makes excellent muffins too. Reduce the amount of bake time to 15-20 minutes.

Morning Glory Muffins

These muffins pack a nutritional punch with wholesome ingredients and delicious flavours. They freeze well so you can easily keep some on hand. Simply allow the muffins to completely cool, then transfer to a large Ziploc bag and store in the freezer.

WET INGREDIENTS

1 cup applesauce
1 cup crushed pineapple
½ cup canola oil
½ cup maple syrup
2 tablespoons lemon juice
1 tablespoon vanilla

DRY INGREDIENTS

3 cups Gluten Free Flour Mix
1 ½ teaspoons baking soda
1 teaspoon guar gum
1 ½ teaspoon cinnamon

ADDITIONAL INGREDIENTS

2 cups shredded carrots
1 cup raisins
½ cup shredded coconut

INSTRUCTIONS

1. Preheat oven to 350° F.
2. Line muffin tin with paper liners, set aside.
3. In a large mixing bowl stir together all wet ingredients.
4. In a separate large mixing bowl, whisk together all dry ingredients.
5. Slowly add dry mixture to the wet mixture, stirring until well incorporated.
6. Gently fold in additional ingredients.
7. Fill muffin liners to the rim with batter.
8. Bake 15 – 20 minutes. Muffins are done when toothpick inserted in the middle comes out clean.
9. Allow muffins to cool 5-10 minutes before transferring to cooling rack.

Banana Chocolate Chip Muffins

There is so much goodness and so much flavour in these muffins. They can easily be eaten for breakfast or snacks. These muffins freeze well, so let them cool and put into a large Ziploc bag to put in your freezer.

INGREDIENTS

1 cup mashed banana
1 teaspoon baking soda

1 cup plain dairy free yogurt
1 tablespoon apple cider vinegar

2 cups Gluten Free Flour Mix
1 teaspoon guar gum
1 cup gluten free quick oats

½ cup maple syrup
2 teaspoons vanilla extract

1 cup dairy free chocolate chips

INSTRUCTIONS

1. Preheat oven to 350° F. Line muffin tin with paper liners, set aside.
2. In a small sized bowl, mash bananas with a fork. Add baking soda, stir and set aside.
3. In another small bowl, add dairy free yogurt and apple cider vinegar, stir to combine and set aside.
4. In a medium sized mixing bowl, add gluten free flour, guar gum and gluten free quick oats; whisk to combine.
5. In another large bowl, add banana mixture, yogurt mixture, maple syrup and vanilla, gently stir until combined.
6. Slowly add wet ingredients to dry ingredients and stir until incorporated.
7. Fill muffin liners almost to the top.
8. Bake 15 – 20 minutes. Muffins are done when toothpick inserted in the middle comes out clean.
9. Allow muffins to cool 5-10 minutes before transferring to cooling rack.

Cranberry Orange Scones

These taste amazing fresh from the oven, with melted vegan margarine as a bonus. The tartness of the cranberries makes a nice contrast to the sweet dough. Are they breakfast? Snack? Dessert? You choose. As far as I'm concerned they make an excellent snack, anytime.

When working with the dough, I always find it easier if I keep my hands slightly damp with water. This helps prevent them from sticking to the dough.

DRY INGREDIENTS
3 cups Gluten Free Flour Mix
⅓ cup white sugar
2 tablespoons baking powder
1 teaspoon guar gum
1 tablespoon orange zest

WET INGREDIENTS
1 cup dairy free yogurt
1 tablespoon lemon juice
½ cup dairy free milk
¼ cup orange juice
⅓ cup canola oil

INSTRUCTIONS
1. Preheat oven to 400° F, line baking sheet with parchment paper, set aside.
2. In a medium sized bowl add all wet ingredients, except oil, whisk to combine, set aside.
3. In a separate bowl, add all dry ingredients, whisk to combine.
4. Add oil and wet mixture to dry mixture, stir until incorporated.
5. Place a sheet of parchment paper on your counter.
6. To shape the scones: divide dough into two equal parts. Shape each portion into a 6-inch round disc.
7. Cut each disc into 6 triangular pieces.
8. Transfer scones to prepared baking sheet.
9. Bake 12-16 minutes. Middle of scones will be soft, but not gooey when done.
10. Let cool for 10 minutes before transferring to a cooling rack.

Cornbread

This is everything you want in a cornbread. It has a light, fluffy texture, a slightly sweet taste and it holds together while being cut and while being eaten.

I experimented so much before coming up with this very successful recipe. So many attempts resulted in a great flavour but never held together. I finally achieved excellent results with a cornbread that tastes great and dosen't fall apart!

It tastes amazing, warm from the oven, topped with some dairy free margarine and drizzled with honey. It also makes a delicious complement to my Molasses Baked Beans.

DRY INGREDIENTS
1 cup cornmeal
½ cup Gluten Free Flour Mix
2 tablespoons sugar
2 teaspoons baking powder
1 teaspoon baking soda
1 teaspoon guar gum

WET INGREDIENTS
1 cup vegan yogurt
¼ cup shortening (melted)
¼ cup dairy free milk of choice

INSTRUCTIONS
1. Preheat oven to 325° F. Lightly grease an 8x8 baking dish.
2. In a large mixing bowl, whisk together all the dry ingredients.
3. Add wet ingredients, one at a time to the dry ingredients.
4. Mix together until thoroughly combined.
5. Evenly spread cornbread mixture into prepared baking dish.
6. Bake for 25-30 minutes. Cornbread is done when toothpick inserted in the centre comes out clean.
7. Let cool before slicing.

Sauces & Dressings

Salad Dressings

I like to keep a variety of dressings on hand so I don't get bored with my salads. It can be hard to find store-bought dressings that are safe to eat. It's a good thing that salad dressings are super easy to make. For each dressing recipe, the steps are the same:

1. Add all ingredients to a blender and blend until combined.
2. Transfer dressing to an airtight container; store in refrigerator.
3. Shake dressing before each use.

DAIRY FREE RANCH DRESSING
INGREDIENTS
½ cup vegan mayonnaise
½ cup canned coconut milk
1 tablespoon apple cider vinegar
½ teaspoon garlic powder
½ teaspoon onion powder
1 teaspoon dried basil
1 teaspoon dried dill

SRIRACHA LIME DRESSING
INGREDIENTS
¼ cup olive oil
¼ cup white wine vinegar
¼ cup honey
3 tablespoons lime juice
1 teaspoon sriracha sauce
½ teaspoon garlic powder
¼ teaspoon salt

SWEET & TANGY SALAD DRESSING
INGREDIENTS
¼ cup olive oil
¼ cup apple cider vinegar
¼ cup maple syrup
½ teaspoon garlic powder
½ teaspoon onion powder
1 teaspoon italian seasoning
1 teaspoon dried dill

CAESAR STYLE DRESSING
INGREDIENTS
½ cup vegan mayonnaise
2 tablespoons lemon juice
1 tablespoon Worcestershire sauce*
1 tablespoon honey
1 tablespoon fish sauce (**or** 1 *teaspoon* salt)
2 tablespoons nutritional yeast
2 teaspoons capers
1 teaspoon minced garlic

*Be sure to carefully read ingredients, as not all Worcestershire sauces are gluten free.

Soy Sauce Alternative

This soy sauce alternative is both soy free and gluten free, and makes an excellent substitute for the real thing. It is probably the strangest recipe that I have experimented with. Trying to come up with a comparable substitute seemed overwhelming. But, I was so excited to finally achieve excellent results.

I like to make up a large batch at a time so smaller portions can be put in the freezer. I tend to freeze it in containers that will hold approximately ¼ of a cup, as many recipes require this quantity. Simply grab a small container or two from the freezer any time you need it.

I use it in a variety of stir fry sauces and other Asian inspired cooking. I have never been disappointed in the results. I use fish sauce for flavouring in this recipe, but to keep it Top 10 free, simply use salt instead.

INGREDIENTS
2 cups chicken broth
2 teaspoons molasses
2 teaspoons balsamic vinegar
1 teaspoon fish sauce
    (*or* ½ teaspoon of salt)

INSTRUCTIONS
1. Combine all ingredients into a small saucepan and bring to a boil.
2. Reduce heat and simmer for 15 minutes.
3. Liquid will reduce slightly.
4. Let sauce cool and store in fridge in an airtight container, or freeze in small batches

Quick & Easy Mayonnaise

There are many excellent vegan options for mayonnaise available, yet many still contain some Top 10 allergens. I always make my own, as it is so easy to do and I control what I put in it.

I use plain vegan yogurt and canola oil in this recipe. The brand I prefer for my food allergies is "Silk Cultured Coconut". Ironically, it does not have a strong coconut flavour. I also choose to use canola oil. You can substitute any plain flavoured dairy free yogurt, and any neutral flavoured oil with similar results.

The mixture is quiet runny when first made, yet sets to an excellent consistency once refrigerated. Use this how you would use any mayonnaise. It can also be used to make a variety of dressings and dips.

INGREDIENTS
½ cup plain vegan yogurt
½ cup canola oil
2 tablespoons lemon juice
1 teaspoon garlic powder
1 teaspoon salt

INSTRUCTIONS
1. Add all ingredients to a tall cup and blend with immersion blender.
2. Store in the refrigerator, in an airtight container.

Awesome Sauce

I love this sauce! I use it on everything. It can be used as a dip, spread or even as salad dressing.

You can adjust the amount of hot sauce to suit your tastes. When you try it, you'll know why the only name I could think to call this is "Awesome Sauce".

INGREDIENTS
¾ cup vegan mayonnaise
¼ cup ketchup
2 tablespoons Worcestershire sauce*
1 tablespoon Frank's Hot Sauce
½ teaspoon pepper

INSTRUCTIONS
1. Add all ingredients to a bowl, and whisk to combine.
2. Store in an airtight container in the fridge.

*Be sure to carefully read ingredients, as not all Worcestershire sauces are gluten free.

Lunch Ideas

Mason Jar Salads

Mason jar salads are a portable meal, with endless taste options. Pick any veggies you like; choose a variety of greens, a variety of proteins, change up the type of dressing for the bottom layer.

Assembling the ingredients in a specific order is essential to maintain the freshness of the salads. Dressing always goes on the bottom. Leafy greens always get put at the top so they are far removed from dressing and other wet ingredients. The middle can be of all sorts of vegetables.

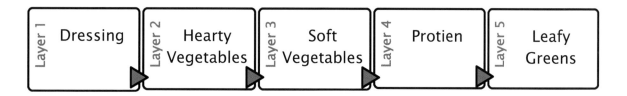

Keep the sealed jars in the refrigerator and they will stay fresh for up to 5 days. Make up a batch on Sunday and then lunches for the week are ready to go.

When it's time to eat, empty the contents of the jar onto a plate, stir to incorporate the dressing and enjoy. Don't forget to pack a fork!

Salad Ideas

CHICKEN RANCH SALAD

1. Dairy Free Ranch Dressing
2. Cucumber
3. Tomato
4. Cooked chicken
5. Spring greens

TACO SALAD

1. Awesome Sauce
2. Red & green peppers
3. Tomatoes
4. Avocado pieces
5. Left over taco meat
6. Romaine lettuce

CHICKEN PASTA SALAD

1. Caesar Style Dressing
2. Cooked gluten free pasta
3. Cooked shredded chicken
4. Cooked crumbled bacon
5. Romaine lettuce

PULLED PORK SALAD

1. Sriracha Lime Dressing
2. Shredded carrots
3. Left over pulled pork
4. Coleslaw mix

SPINACH SALAD

1. Sweet and Tangy Dressing
2. Apple pieces
3. Chopped red onion
4. Dried cranberries
5. Spinach

STRAWBERRY KALE SALAD

1. Sweet & Tangy Dressing
2. Sliced radishes
3. Sliced strawberries
4. Shredded kale

Main Meals - Chicken

Easy Fried Chicken

This is a simple family recipe of mine. My mother has Celiac disease, so this is how I learned to make fried chicken. It continues to be the easiest and most tasty fried chicken.

I like to flatten the chicken breasts so they cook quickly and evenly. Starch is used to make a delicious crispy coating. I have used potato starch, cornstarch and arrowroot flour with great success. Use the starch that works best for your allergy needs.

Cooking the chicken pieces on both sides, with a small amount of oil on the bottom of a large skillet, is all that is required to make the chicken crispy and golden.

INGREDIENTS

4-6 boneless, skinless chicken breasts
2 cups potato starch (or other starch)
1 teaspoon black pepper
1 teaspoon garlic powder
½ teaspoon cayenne pepper
½ teaspoon salt
Oil for frying

INSTRUCTIONS

1. Flatten chicken pieces to approximately ¼" thickness between two pieces of plastic wrap or wax paper, set aside.
2. Add starch and seasonings to a large Ziploc bag.
3. Seal the bag and toss to mix seasonings into the starch.
4. Heat 2-3 tablespoons of oil in a large skillet.
5. Add one piece of chicken at a time to the Ziploc bag; ensure chicken is well coated.
6. Shake off excess starch, place in frying pan.
7. Repeat with remainder of chicken, cooking in several batches as to not overcrowd.
8. Cook chicken on both sides until golden brown, approximately 8-10 minutes per side.
9. Set cooked pieces on a plate lined with paper towel, to absorb any excess oil.

Sticky Orange Chicken

This chicken recipe makes an excellent substitute for Chinese food take out. It has a light and crispy coating, with a delicious sweet and sour sauce. Freshly squeezed orange juice taste the best, yet feel free to use what you have on hand; it will still taste amazing.

My Soy Sauce Alternative works perfectly when making this sauce.

INGREDIENTS
3-4 skinless, boneless chicken breasts
2/3 cup cornstarch
Oil for frying

FOR THE SAUCE:
½ cup orange juice
1 tablespoon orange zest
¼ cup soy sauce alternative
¼ cup rice wine vinegar
½ cup brown sugar
½ teaspoon garlic
¼ teaspoon ginger

TO THICKEN THE SAUCE:
2 tablespoons cornstarch
2 tablespoons cold water

Use cold water when making cornstarch slurry to avoid clumping.

INSTRUCTIONS
1. Slice chicken into 1" sized cubes; add pieces to a large Ziploc bag.
2. Add cornstarch, seal the bag & toss to coat chicken with cornstarch.
3. Heat 2-3 tablespoons of oil in a large skillet.
4. Add chicken pieces, be careful not to overcrowd. Cook in two separate batches if necessary.
5. Brown chicken on both sides cooking until internal temperature reaches 165° F (approximately 6-8 minutes per side)
6. Transfer cooked chicken to a plate covered with paper towel.
7. Add all sauce ingredients to the skillet, whisk to combine, bring to a gentle boil.
8. Prepare cornstarch slurry; mixing equal parts cornstarch and cold water.
9. Add slurry to sauce, continue stirring until sauce thickens; reduce heat.
10. Transfer chicken back into skillet with sauce, and stir until all chicken pieces are thoroughly covered in sauce.

Crispy Chicken Tenders

These chicken tenders are juicy on the inside, light and crispy on the outside. I use gluten free cereals to make crumbs - a mixture of Rice Chex and Crispix is my favourite combination. Add cereal to a large Ziploc bag and crush with a rolling pin. If preferred, make crumbs with a food processor. For a sweet variation, add ½ cup sweetened, shredded coconut to the crumb mixture.

To make dairy free buttermilk, simply add 1 tablespoon of lemon juice or apple cider vinegar to your choice of dairy free milk. Plain vegan yogurt, thinned with a bit of water can also be used instead of buttermilk.

INGREDIENTS

3-4 boneless, skinless chicken breasts
2 cups gluten free crumbs
½ cup dairy free buttermilk or thinned plain vegan yogurt
¼ teaspoon onion powder
¼ teaspoon garlic powder
¼ teaspoon black pepper
¼ teaspoon seasoned salt
Oil for frying

INSTRUCTIONS

1. Slice chicken into 1" thick strips, lengthwise, set aside.
2. Place a large skillet on the stove; add 2-3 tablespoons of oil, heat to medium high.
3. Add buttermilk (or thinned plain vegan yogurt) and seasonings to a shallow dish, stir to combine.
4. Add crumbs to another shallow dish.
5. Working with one piece at a time, dredge the chicken in the buttermilk, then the gluten free crumb mixture, ensuring all sides are covered with the batter.
6. Add coated chicken strips to the oil without overcrowding.
7. Brown chicken on both sides, cooking until an internal temperature of 165° F is reached. (approximately 6-8 minutes per side)
8. Remove cooked chicken and place on a wire cooling rack placed over paper towels. This helps keep the coating on the chicken pieces.

Creamy Italian Chicken

This chicken dish is fancy enough to serve to company, yet simple enough to make for a delicious weeknight meal. No one would guess that the rich and creamy sauce is dairy free.

For my dairy free milk of choice, I like to use one can of coconut milk. I empty the can into bowl and whisk it until the cream and liquid are nicely combined. This gives the milk a smooth and creamy consistency.

You can use 2 cups of any plain flavoured dairy free milk of your choice.

INGREDIENTS

6-8 slices of bacon
3-4 boneless, skinless chicken breasts
1 medium onion, sliced
2-3 cups sliced mushrooms
2 cups plain, dairy free milk
1-2 tablespoons olive oil
1 tablespoon minced garlic
2 teaspoons italian seasoning
1 teaspoon dried thyme
½ teaspoon black pepper
½ teaspoon salt

INSTRUCTIONS

1. Sprinkle both sides of chicken with italian seasoning, set aside.
2. Cook bacon until crispy, remove from pan and let drain on some paper towel. Crumble once cooled.
3. Drain bacon grease from pan, add chicken breasts.
4. Cook chicken until internal temperature reaches 165° F, approximately 6-8 minutes per side.
5. Remove chicken from pan, set aside.
6. Add olive oil and minced garlic to pan, sauté until aromatic; approximately 1 minute.
7. Add sliced onions and sauté until softened, approximately 2-4 minutes.
8. Add mushrooms and continue to sauté until softened, approximately 2-4 minutes.
9. Add milk, thyme and black pepper and salt, gently stirring until incorporated.
10. Return chicken to pan, add crumbled bacon.
11. Heat until chicken is warm again; adjust seasonings to taste.

Sweet & Spicy Bacon Wrapped Chicken

Everything tastes better with bacon! This is so simple to make and a hit with people of all ages. I like this chicken best when grilled on the BBQ, yet it also works well cooked in the oven.

The bacon is wrapped around the chicken, so you will need about two pieces of bacon per chicken breast. Thinly sliced bacon works best when using it to wrap around meat.

INGREDIENTS

4 boneless, skinless chicken breasts
8 slices of bacon
1-2 teaspoons paprika **or** chili powder
¼ cup brown sugar

INSTRUCTIONS

1. Lightly oil a 8x11 casserole dish, preheat oven to 400° F, or preheat BBQ to 400° F.
2. Sprinkle both sides of chicken with paprika **or** chili powder.
3. Place brown sugar in a shallow dish.
4. Wrap bacon around chicken, one piece at a time.
5. Dip wrapped chicken in the brown sugar, coating both sides, place on plate or prepared casserole dish.
6. Pace dish in oven and cook until internal temperature reaches 165° F; approximately 20 minutes.
7. Or, place chicken on grill and cook each side for approximately 6-8 minutes, until internal temperature reaches 165° F

Buffalo Chicken Meatballs

These meatballs provide a healthier option to chicken wings, while still packing a nice flavourful punch. Adjust the amount of hot sauce to suit your tastes. I use plain potato flakes as a binder. Leftover mashed potatoes work very well too. You may have to adjust the amount of potato to account for varying moisture levels of the ground chicken. You need enough potato to help the meatballs maintain shape.

Make smaller meatballs to serve as an appetizer, or larger ones to use as a meal. Serve with extra hot sauce and/or some dairy free sour cream for an added flavour boost.

INGREDIENTS
1 pound ground chicken
½ cups plain potato flakes
¼ cup Frank's Red Hot Sauce

INSTRUCTIONS
1. Line a baking sheet with parchment paper, preheat oven to 400° F.
2. Combine all ingredients in a medium sized mixing bowl, and mix well.
3. Shape into desired size meatballs.
4. Cook 12-18 minutes, depending on size of meatballs. Cook until an internal temperature of 165° F is reached.

Main Meals - Pork

Slow Cooker Pulled Pork

Pulled pork is one of my favourite meals. It is so easy to prepare, freezes well, makes great leftovers and can sit in a slow cooker on "warm" for hours and still taste amazing. Serve it over rice, potatoes or any side you like. The steps to these two recipes are similar. Only the method of adding the sauce ingredients is different, as indicated.

APPLE BUTTER PULLED PORK
INGREDIENTS
2-3 pound pork roast
½ cup balsamic vinegar
½ cup apple butter
½ cup water
2 tablespoons molasses
1 teaspoon garlic powder
½ teaspoon black pepper
½ teaspoon salt

INSTRUCTIONS
1. Rinse pork and place in the bottom of slow cooker.
2. Combine all sauce ingredients in a small sized bowl, whisk to combine.
3. Pour sauce over pork roast.
4. Set slow cooker on low and cook for 5-7 hours.
5. Remove pork from slow cooker, set on a plate or cutting board. Shred pork using two forks.
6. Place shredded pork back into slow cooker and toss with the sauce.

SMOKED PULLED PORK
INGREDIENTS
2-3 pound pork roast
3-4 tablespoons liquid smoke
Coarse Himalayan Pink Salt

INSTRUCTIONS
1. Add liquid smoke to the bottom of the slow cooker.
2. Rinse pork and place in the bottom of slow cooker.
3. Sprinkle both sides of pork with Himalayan Pink Salt (coarse ground works best)

Steps **4-6** are the same as above.

Himalayan Pink Salt gives a superior flavour to table salt.

Maple Sriracha Pork Tenderloin

This recipe creates a juicy and tender roast with a well-balanced sweet and tangy sauce.

The moisture inside the roast needs time to redistribute through the meat once it has finished cooking. Letting it rest for 5-10 minutes before slicing will cause the meat to become juicy and tender.

INGREDIENTS
2 ½ pounds pork tenderloin
1 tablespoon seasoning salt
¼ cup olive oil
¼ cup soy sauce alternative
¼ cup maple syrup
1 tablespoons sriracha sauce
3 tablespoons orange juice
1 tablespoon lime juice

INSTRUCTIONS
1. Lightly oil a 9x13 casserole dish, and preheat oven to 350° F.
2. Rinse tenderloin with cold water, pat dry with paper towel and place in prepared casserole dish.
3. Sprinkle both sides of tenderloin with seasoning salt.
4. In a small sized mixing bowl, whisk together all remaining ingredients.
5. Gently pour sauce around tenderloin.
6. Cook uncovered until internal temperature reaches 145° F, approximately 40-50 minutes.
7. Remove pan from oven, transfer tenderloin to a cutting board and allow pork to rest 5-10 minutes before slicing.
8. While pork is resting, make a glaze from the leftover liquid by pouring rendered liquid into a small sauce pan, bringing to a gentle boil and letting simmer until liquid has slightly thickened, approximately 8-10 minutes.

Pork Schnitzel

To make classic pork schnitzel, you need flour, egg wash and crumbs. To make this Top 10 Free, I use starch instead of flour, dairy free yogurt to replace the egg, and gluten free cereal for crumbs.

I have used potato starch, cornstarch and arrowroot starch with great success. I use a mixture of Rice Chex and Crispix to make gluten free crumbs.

INGREDIENTS

4 boneless pork chops, ½ inch thick
½ cup of starch
1 teaspoon seasoning salt
½ teaspoon black pepper
½ cup plain dairy free yogurt
2 cups gluten free crumbs
Oil for frying

INSTRUCTIONS

1. Using a meat mallet, pound pork chops to ¼ - ⅛ inch thickness.
2. Cut tiny slits around the edges of the meat to prevent curing while cooking.
3. In one shallow bowl, add the starch, seasoning salt and pepper; whisk to combine.
4. In a second shallow bowl add dairy free yogurt diluted with some water until it has a similar consistency to an egg wash.
5. In a third shallow bowl, add gluten free crumbs. To make the crumbs, add gluten free cereal to a large Ziploc bag and crush with a rolling pin.
6. Heat 2-3 tablespoons of oil in a large skillet on medium high heat.
7. Working one piece at a time, dredge the pork first in the seasoned starch, then in the dairy free yogurt, then in the gluten free crumbs.
8. Add to the skillet and sauté for 3-4 minutes per side.
9. Remove pork from the skillet and place on a wire cooling rack. This helps keep the coating on the pork pieces.

Maple Glazed Ham

Baked ham makes a simple, low maintenance main dish. The maple glaze turns a basic ham into a deliciously sticky and sweet delight. I have yet to find anyone who doesn't love this ham recipe – both adults and kids.

I have included oven and Instant Pot instructions. Using the Instant Pot allows the oven to be used for other dishes if you are making a holiday feast!

INGREDIENTS

1 spiral sliced fully cooked ham
½ cup maple syrup
½ cup brown sugar
¼ teaspoon ground cloves

Note: This makes enough glaze for a 3-5 pound ham. Double the ingredients to make more glaze for a larger sized ham. You can never have too much glaze!

OVEN INSTRUCTIONS

1. Preheat oven to 300° F. Place ham on a rack in a shallow roasting pan. Cover and bake for 10 minutes per pound or until a thermometer reads 130° F.
2. Meanwhile, in a large saucepan, combine glaze ingredients. Bring to a boil; cook and stir until slightly thickened, 2-3 minutes.
3. Remove ham from oven. Pour glaze over ham. Bake ham, uncovered, until a thermometer reads 140° F, about 15-30 minutes longer.

Maple Glazed Ham

INSTANT POT INSTRUCTIONS:

1. Place trivet inside the inner pot of instant pot, pour in 1 cup of water.
2. Place ham on a large sheet of heavy-duty aluminum foil; fold up the sides to shape around the ham.
3. Gently separate slices of spiral ham, so glaze can penetrate the ham slices.
4. Pour maple syrup over ham, then sprinkle with the brown sugar and ground cloves.
5. Securely wrap foil around the ham, and place into prepared instant pot.
6. Set Instant pot to pressure cook on high for 2 minutes per pound; quick release when done.

Optional: Reduce liquid to thicken into glaze:

1. Place foil packed ham on heat safe surface. Gently open foil, remove ham to a large platter.
2. Remove trivet and discard water.
3. Place inner pot back onto Instant Pot, set to "sauté". Carefully pour rendered liquid into pot.
4. Create slurry by combining 1 tablespoon of cornstarch with 1 tablespoon of cold water.
5. Add slurry to rendered liquid, whisk well, and cook until the glaze is reduced by half, about 3-4 minutes.
6. Pour the thickened glaze over the ham.

10 minutes of extra cooking time is needed to account for heating through heavy-duty tin foil. So, cook time will be 10 minutes *plus* 2 minutes per pound.

Main Meals - Beef

Sheet Pan Fajitas

Sheet pan fajitas make a simple, quick and delicious meal. This meal takes about 15-20 minutes to cook in the oven, all on one baking tray. You can serve this over rice, wrap in soft tortillas, or place into crunchy taco shells. I haven't found a soft tortilla that I can eat, so I enjoy using taco shells. You can also choose the meat you prefer. Chicken and beef both taste delicious with the simple marinade.

INGREDIENTS

1 ½ pounds meat of choice, cut into thin strips
3 bell peppers, any combo of colours
1 medium onion
3 tablespoons olive oil
3 tablespoons lime juice
½ teaspoon chili powder
½ teaspoon cumin
¼ teaspoon salt

INSTRUCTIONS

1. Lightly brush baking tray with oil. Preheat oven to 400° F.
2. Cut chicken or beef into thin strips; add to a large mixing bowl.
3. Slice peppers and onions into thin strips; add to same bowl.
4. Add olive oil, lime juice and seasonings to same bowl, tossing meat and vegetables to thoroughly coat.
5. Transfer everything to prepared tray; spreading evenly.
6. Place in oven, on middle rack, cook until meat reaches proper internal temperature, approximately 15-20 minutes.
7. Serve over rice, in wraps, or taco shells.

Slow Cooker Mongolian Beef

This recipe is so simple to prepare and will become a new family favourite. Using the slow cooker eases a lot of work. Add this to your weeknight supper rotation for a low maintenance, delicious meal.

I toss the beef in cornstarch before putting it in the slow cooker. This helps keep the moisture locked in the meat. Use whichever starch best suits your allergy needs.

I like to serve this over wide rice noodles. Try it over rice, potatoes or your favourite pasta.

INGREDIENTS
1 pound sliced flank steak
¼ cup cornstarch
½ cup water
½ cup soy sauce alternative
⅔ cup brown sugar
1 tablespoon minced garlic
½ teaspoon minced ginger

INSTRUCTIONS
1. Add cornstarch to a large Ziploc bag, set aside.
2. Slice flank steak against the grain to ¼" thick pieces.
3. Add beef to Ziploc bag and toss to fully coat each piece of meat.
4. In a medium sized mixing bowl add all remaining ingredients, whisk to combine.
5. Dump the beef from the Ziploc bag into the slow cooker.
6. Gently pour in sauce.
7. Cook for 4-5 hours on low or 2-3 on high.

Classic Meatloaf

It is a challenge to find a suitable binder for meatloaf without wheat or eggs. Both eggs and bread soaked in milk are often used to provide stability and moisture. One or the other can be left out, but certainly not both or the meatloaf will just fall apart.

I have tried using either potato flakes, left over mashed potatoes or gluten free quick oats; all with great success.

If you have an Instant Pot, it can be used to cook meatloaf allowing this to become a possible week night meal. I have included both oven and Instant Pot instructions.

INGREDIENTS
1 ½ pounds ground beef
1 small onion, diced
¼ cup ketchup
2 tablespoons Worcestershire sauce*
1 teaspoon italian seasoning
⅓ cup mashed potato, potato flakes or gluten free quick oats.

Be sure to carefully read ingredients, as not all Worcestershire sauces are gluten free.

OVEN INSTRUCTIONS
1. Add all ingredients to a medium sized mixing bowl. Use your hands to thoroughly combine.
2. If cooking in conventional oven, preheat to 350° F, and pack mixture into a lightly oiled loaf pan.
3. Cook until internal temperature reaches 160°F, approximately 50-60 minutes.

INSTANT POT INSTRUCTIONS
1. Create a "pan" from heavy duty tin foil, and pack meat into loaf form.
2. Place trivet on bottom of Instant Pot, add 1 cup water.
3. Place meatloaf within its tin foil pan onto trivet.
4. Pressure cook for 23 minutes on high.
5. Use either quick release or natural release, depending on your time requirements.
6. Lift trivet, along with tin foil pan and place on large plate or dish.
7. Unwrap tin foil, slice and serve meatloaf.

Tacos

Tacos always make a quick and easy meal. Cook and season the beef and prepare a variety of toppings. Everyone can choose to add what they want. I don't worry about a cheese substitute for myself as other toppings are satisfying to me. I love adding sliced avocado to my tacos for delicious flavour and creaminess.

I make my own taco seasoning, and like to keep a batch in my panty. You can adjust the seasonings according to your taste preferences. It is as simple as adding the spices to a mason jar or other airtight container and shaking to combine.

When it comes time to make tacos, simply cook and drain your meat, add some pre-made taco seasoning and water and you're ready to eat!

INGREDIENTS FOR TACO SEASONING
½ cup chili powder
¼ cup onion powder
2 tablespoons cumin
1 tablespoon paprika
1 tablespoon garlic powder
1 tablespoon salt

Add all spices to a mason jar or other airtight container and shake to combine.

Tacos

INGREDIENTS FOR TACO MEAT

1 pound lean ground beef

2-3 tablespoons Taco Seasoning

¼ cup water

INSTRUCTIONS FOR TACO MEAT

1. Place ground beef in a large skillet and cook over medium heat until cooked.
2. Drain excess oil from pan.
3. Add taco seasoning and water, stirring until well combined.
4. Adjust seasonings to taste.
5. Serve in hard or soft shells.
6. Add any toppings you wish!

Main Meals - Pasta & More

Roasted Red Pepper Sauce

This roasted red pepper pasta sauce is super creamy and delicious. It has a slightly sweet flavour with a touch of spice. I use Frank's Original Red Hot Sauce as an excellent complement to the sweetness of the roasted red peppers. Adjust the amount used to suit your tastes.

INGREDIENTS

Gluten free pasta of your choice
2 red bell peppers
1 small onion
2 tablespoons olive oil
2-3 teaspoons minced garlic
2-3 tablespoons nutritional yeast
2 tablespoons Frank's original hot sauce
¼ teaspoon red pepper flakes (optional)
1 can coconut milk (or 1 ½ cups plain, dairy free milk of choice)
Salt & pepper to taste

Sauce can be made ahead of time and frozen.

INSTRUCTIONS

1. Lightly brush baking sheet with oil, preheat oven to 425° F.
2. Dice red peppers and onions, place in large mixing bowl.
3. Add olive oil and minced garlic to peppers and onions, toss to coat.
4. Spread peppers and onions onto prepared baking sheet.
5. Cook peppers and onions until tender, approximately 20 minutes.
6. While peppers and onions are cooking, add dairy free milk, nutritional yeast, hot sauce and seasonings to a blender, set aside.
7. Bring a medium pot of water to a boil, add gluten free pasta and cook according to package instructions. Drain once cooked, set aside.
8. Once peppers and onions are cooked, allow to cool slightly, then transfer to blender with other ingredients, and blend all ingredients until smooth.
9. Add blended sauce to a large pot or skillet, and warm on low heat, adjust seasonings to taste.
10. Add cooked pasta, and toss to coat.

"Cheesy" Pasta Sauce

In my opinion, nothing can replace the taste of real cheese. However, it is still possible to make a deliciously creamy sauce that is very reminiscent of the real thing. Pour this sauce over any of your favourite allergen safe noodles for a comforting meal.

This sauce also makes an excellent nacho dip! So, when you next gather with friends, grab a couple of bags of gluten free tortilla chips, whip up a batch of this sauce and watch in delight as your guests devour the sauce, never guessing it is dairy free.

INGREDIENTS
Gluten free pasta of your choice
1 ½ cups chopped potato
½ cup chicken broth
½ cup plain, dairy free milk
2 tablespoons canola oil
¼ cup nutritional yeast
½ teaspoon garlic powder
1 teaspoon salt
¼ teaspoon turmeric powder

INSTRUCTIONS
1. Cook your favourite gluten free pasta according to package directions, drain & set aside.
2. Peel & chop potatoes, add to a medium sauce pan, cover with water and bring to a boil. Cook potatoes until tender, approximately 15 minutes. Drain excess water.
3. Add all remaining ingredients plus the drained potatoes to a blender and blend until smooth.
4. Pour sauce over cooked pasta and toss thoroughly.

Sauce can be made ahead of time and frozen.

Avocado Spinach Pasta Sauce

Two super foods combine to make a rich, creamy and flavourful sauce. Spinach and avocado both have many nutritional benefits. It's a bonus that they come together in a delicious way in this sauce.

This is so quick and easy to make that supper can be ready in a hurry. It also has a taste to impress, so can easily be served to wow company at a dinner party.

INGREDIENTS
Gluten free pasta of your choice
2 avocados
2 cups baby spinach
2 teaspoons minced garlic
⅓ cup olive oil
2 tablespoons lemon juice
Salt and pepper to taste

INSTRUCTIONS
1. Bring a medium pot of water to a boil, add gluten free pasta and cook according to package instructions. Drain once cooked, set aside.
2. Add all sauce ingredients to a food processor or blender; blend until smooth.
3. Add blended sauce to a large pot or skillet, and warm on low heat, adjust seasonings to taste.
4. Add cooked pasta, and toss to coat.

Sauce can be made ahead of time and frozen.

Molasses Baked Beans

This is my favourite slow cooker recipe. I love how it smells as it cooks, and it takes just a few minutes to prepare. It's so nice to come home to a warm and comforting meal.

Cornbread makes an excellent complement to a bowl of molasses baked beans.

INGREDIENTS

3 cans pinto beans
½ cup molasses
½ cup water
¼ cup brown sugar
2 tablespoons Worcestershire sauce

INSTRUCTIONS

1. Drain and rinse beans and place into slow cooker.
2. In a small bowl whisk together all remaining ingredients, and pour over beans.
3. Cook on Low for 7-9 hours or High for 4-5 hours.

Be sure to carefully read ingredients, as not all Worcestershire sauces are gluten free.

Side Dishes

Cornbread Stuffing

Dried out cubes of cornbread are required before making this stuffing. So, make up a double batch of Cornbread – one to eat and one to turn into stuffing. To dry out the cornbread for stuffing, cut a batch into bite sized cubes. Spread evenly on a baking sheet and allow to dry overnight. Or, you can put the baking sheet in the oven and bake at 200° F for about 90 minutes. Then proceed to follow the ingredient list and instructions to make the stuffing.

This recipe uses vegan margarine. There are many varieties of vegan margarine available. Be sure to choose one that is safe for your allergies

INGREDIENTS

1 batch of Cornbread, cubed and dried
¼ cup vegan margarine
2-3 cups chicken broth
1 large sweet onion, diced
4 stalks of celery, diced
1 teaspoon thyme
1 teaspoon rosemary
½ teaspoon sage
½ teaspoon salt

INSTRUCTIONS

1. Preheat oven to 350° F, lightly oil a 9x13 casserole dish, set aside.
2. Melt vegan margarine in a large skillet on the stove over medium heat.
3. Add diced onions, celery and spices. Cook over medium heat until tender, not browned.
4. Place dried cornbread cubes into prepared casserole dish. Add cooked onion and celery mixture.
5. Slowly add chicken broth, 1 cup at a time, gently stirring. The mixture needs to be moist, not soggy.
6. Bake 25-30 minutes, until top is golden brown.

Oven Baked Fries

Good old-fashioned oven fries are simple, versatile and make a delicious side dish. You can slice the potatoes in wedges, shoe string or even diced. Feel free to change up the spices to try different flavours. I have kept the spice simple for this basic recipe as it suits so many taste preferences.

Different potatoes will have different flavours, so try a variety to keep things interesting. I like russet potatoes best for making oven baked fries.

INGREDIENTS
3-4 russet potatoes
2-3 tablespoons olive oil
½ teaspoon salt
½ teaspoon pepper
½ teaspoon garlic powder

INSTRUCTIONS
1. Preheat oven to 425° F. Line baking tray with parchment paper.
2. Chop potatoes into strips or wedges; add to a large mixing bowl.
3. Add oil and seasonings to potatoes, toss to coat.
4. Spread fries evenly on prepared baking tray.
5. Bake until golden brown, approximately 30 minutes.

Roasted Root Vegetables

I love the simplicity and variety of roasting vegetables in the oven. You can choose any variety of vegetables and any combination of spices to meet any taste preference. The only trick to cooking a number of different vegetables at the same time is to cut them all roughly the same size. This way they will take the same length of time to cook. You will end up with a sheet pan filled with tender, lightly seasoned vegetables making an excellent complement to any meal.

INGREDIENTS

3 pounds assorted root vegetables, chopped into 1 ½" pieces
3 tablespoons olive oil
3 teaspoon dried rosemary
2 teaspoons dried thyme
1 teaspoon salt
½ teaspoon pepper

INSTRUCTIONS

1. Preheat oven to 400° F and line a baking sheet with parchment paper. Set aside.
2. Peel and chop all vegetables, add to a large mixing bowl.
3. Add olive oil and seasonings, toss to thoroughly coat all vegetables.
4. Spread vegetables evenly over prepared baking sheet.
5. Bake for 35-45 minutes, turning the vegetables with a spatula halfway through cooking. Vegetables are finished roasting once they are tender when pierced with a fork.

Warm Potato Salad

This is more commonly referred to as German Potato Salad. The dressing is made with tangy oil and vinegar dressing, not mayonnaise. I like to add spinach to the potato salad for extra flavour and nutrition. It can be made without spinach and still be equally delicious.

The potato salad is meant to be eaten warm, but I have enjoyed it as cold leftovers many times. I sometimes find it easier to cook the potatoes ahead of time, and cook the bacon and dressing just before eating.

INGREDIENTS
1 ½ pounds of potatoes
6-8 slices bacon
¼ cup apple cider vinegar
2 tablespoons olive oil
2 tablespoons sugar
¼ teaspoon salt
½ teaspoon pepper
4 cups baby spinach

INSTRUCTIONS
1. Peel and chop potatoes into ¾ cubes, place in medium sized pot.
2. Cover potatoes with water, bring to a boil, and reduce to a medium heat once boiling.
3. Cook potatoes until fork tender, approximately 20 minutes. Once cooked, drain potatoes and transfer to a large mixing bowl.
4. While potatoes are boiling, cook bacon until crispy.
5. Remove bacon from skillet, place on paper towel to drain. Chop into bite sized portions once cool.
6. Drain all but 2 tablespoons of bacon grease from skillet, return skillet to stove.
7. On low heat add olive oil, vinegar, sugar, salt and pepper to the skillet.
8. Whisk dressing until sugar is dissolved, transfer dressing to heat safe dish.
9. Add spinach to skillet, keeping on low heat. Cook spinach just until wilted. The spinach will shrink in size considerably when wilted.
10. Add spinach and chopped bacon to the cooked potatoes.
11. Taste dressing and adjust seasonings according to taste.
12. Pour dressing over potatoes, bacon and spinach; toss to coat.

Scalloped Potatoes

Creamy, smooth and tender scalloped potatoes made without dairy – amazing. These can make an everyday meal feel special. Add this to your holiday feast menu for a side dish everyone can enjoy. Nothing can precisely replace real cheese, but wow, the sauce used in this recipe is delicious! No one will miss the cheese.

INGREDIENTS

5 cups sliced potatoes
2 cups dairy free milk, plain unsweetened
1 cup chicken broth
⅓ cup nutritional yeast
1 teaspoon garlic powder
1 teaspoon onion powder
½ teaspoon dried thyme
½ teaspoon salt
¼ teaspoon cayenne pepper

Cornstarch Slurry:
¼ cup cornstarch
¼ cup cold water

Use cold water when making cornstarch slurry to avoid clumping.

INSTRUCTIONS

1. Peel and thinly slice the potatoes – using the fine slice blade on a food processor makes very quick work of this.
2. Submerge your potato slices in a bowl of cold water to prevent oxidation.
3. Preheat the oven to 425° F, lightly oil a casserole dish, approximately 9x13.
4. In a medium pot, whisk together the milk, chicken broth, nutritional yeast, and spices. Bring the sauce mixture to a simmer, stirring frequently.
5. In a small bowl, mix together the cornstarch and cold water until there are no clumps.
6. Pour the cornstarch slurry into the simmering sauce and whisk well. When thickened, remove the pot from heat.
7. Drain the potatoes. Layer half in the casserole dish; pour half the sauce over the potatoes. Continue to layer the remaining potatoes and sauce.
8. Cover the dish with foil and bake for 25 minutes. Uncover and bake for an additional 15-20 minutes – or until the potatoes are fork tender.

Mashed Potatoes

Mashed potatoes typically get mixed with cream and butter to give them rich flavour. There is a simple and healthier alternative to make dairy free mashed potatoes. Cooking potatoes in chicken broth instead of water, and adding optional garlic are what I rely on for flavourful, fluffy mashed potatoes. Another alternative is to add vegan margarine when mashing the potatoes. Be sure to read all food labels, ensuring margarine is safe for your food allergy needs.

INGREDIENTS
2-3 pounds of potatoes
Chicken broth
Minced garlic
Vegan margarine
Salt
Pepper

INSTRUCTIONS
1. Peel and chop desired amount of potatoes.
2. Add chopped potatoes to medium sized pot. Add chicken broth until potatoes are covered with liquid.
3. For optional extra flavour, add 1 tablespoon of minced garlic to pot.
4. Bring to a boil and cook until potatoes are fork tender, approximately 15-20 minutes.
5. Once cooked, drain broth into a separate bowl, keep potatoes in the pot.
6. Begin mashing potatoes, adding drained broth and vegan margarine until desired consistency is reached.
7. Add salt and pepper to taste.

Chicken Gravy

Gravy is such a basic condiment, yet often calls for flour, butter, milk or some combination of those ingredients. Many gravy recipes are made with drippings from a roast. I have learned an incredibly easy method to make gravy from scratch. This gravy is dairy free and gluten free. It can be made without relying on drippings from a roast. Try making this gravy to accompany your homemade fried chicken and mashed potatoes.

This recipe uses vegan margarine instead of butter. There are many varieties of vegan margarine available. Be sure to choose one that is safe for your allergies.

INGREDIENTS

2 cups chicken stock
¼ cup vegan margarine
¼ teaspoon onion powder
½ teaspoon garlic powder
½ teaspoon pepper
¼ teaspoon salt

Cornstarch Slurry:
¼ cup cornstarch
¼ cup cold water

INSTRUCTIONS

1. Add chicken broth to a saucepan, bring to a gentle boil.
2. Whisk all spices into broth, add margarine.
3. Continue to cook until margarine melts throughout.
4. Create slurry to thicken gravy by mixing cornstarch and cold water in a small glass or bowl.
5. Add slurry to gravy, whisk to combine. Continue whisking until gravy thickens.

Use cold water when making cornstarch slurry to avoid clumping.

Sweets & Treats

Coffee Crumb Cake

A classic coffee cake made Top 10 Free. It is light and fluffy, with the right amount of crumble on top. I have brought this to countless potlucks and meetings. Everyone is always so surprised to find it is free from common allergens.

This recipe uses vegan margarine instead of butter. There are many varieties of vegan margarine available. Be sure to choose one that is safe for your allergies.

CRUMB TOPPING INGREDIENTS
½ cup gluten free oat flour
½ cup brown sugar
½ teaspoon cinnamon
¼ cup vegan margarine

WET CAKE INGREDIENTS
1 cup plain dairy free yogurt
1 tablespoon apple cider vinegar
½ cup maple syrup
½ cup vegan margarine

DRY CAKE INGREDIENTS
2 cups Gluten Free Flour Mix
1 teaspoon baking powder
1 teaspoon baking soda
½ teaspoon guar gum

CRUMB TOPPING INSTRUCTIONS
1. Whisk together gluten free oat flour, brown sugar and cinnamon.
2. Add chilled vegan margarine and stir until pea sized clumps form, set aside.

CAKE INSTRUCTIONS
1. Lightly oil a 9x9 cake pan, preheat oven to 325° F
2. In a small bowl, add dairy free yogurt, stir in apple cider vinegar, set aside.
3. In a separate bowl, whisk to combine maple syrup and vegan margarine, set aside.
4. In a large mixing bowl, add all dry ingredients and whisk to combine.
5. Add margarine mix and yogurt mix to the dry ingredients, stir until incorporated.
6. Pour cake mixture into prepared cake pan.
7. Smooth surface with a wet spatula, to prevent it from sticking to the cake batter.
8. Sprinkle crumb topping evenly over the top.
9. Bake 35-40 minutes, until top is golden and the cake is no longer wet in the centre.

Mixed Berry Crumble

It's hard to go wrong with a berry crumble for dessert. Simple ingredients come together to make a delicious and comforting dessert. You can use a combination of any berries, or all of one kind if you prefer. Add some diced rhubarb when it is in season for a nice variety.

Fresh berries work best, yet if frozen is what you have, don't let that stop you from making something delicious. It will be easier to work with them if you keep them frozen. You may have to increase bake time by just a few minutes.

BERRY FILLING INGREDIENTS
4 cups of berries
¼ cup white sugar
2 tablespoons Gluten Free Flour Mix

CRUMBLE INGREDIENTS
1 cup gluten free oats
½ cup Gluten Free Flour Mix
½ cup brown sugar
½ cup vegan margarine

INSTRUCTIONS
1. Preheat oven to 350° F, lightly oil a 8x11 casserole dish, set aside.
2. Wash and gently dry fresh berries. If using frozen berries; keep them frozen.
3. In a medium sized mixing bowl, add berries, white sugar and 2 tablespoons of gluten free flour mix, use a wooden spoon to gently combine, set aside.
4. In a separate bowl, whisk together brown sugar and gluten free oats.
5. Add vegan margarine or shortening, and stir until combined; small clumps are normal.
6. Place half of the crumb mixture on the bottom of the prepare casserole dish.
7. Place all the berry filling on top of the crumb mixture
8. Place remaining crumb mixture on top of the berry filling.
9. Bake for 25-35 minutes, until the crumble on top is golden brown.

Chocolate Pudding

Avocados are the key ingredient to making this creamy and smooth chocolate pudding. It is probably the quickest dessert to make, ever. All you need to do is blend the few ingredients together. You can adjust the amount of cocoa powder, dairy free milk and maple syrup depending on your desired taste and consistency. A superfood turned into a dessert? What could be better?

INGREDIENTS

2 ripe avocados
½ cup cocoa powder
¼ cup dairy free milk
¼ cup maple syrup

INSTRUCTIONS

1. Cut avocado in half, throw away pit.
2. Scoop the flesh into a blender.
3. Add remaining ingredients, and blend until smooth.
4. Taste and add more maple syrup and/or cocoa powder if desired.
5. Add more milk to make a thinner consistency, if desired.

Oat Flour Pie Crust

This oat flour pie crust is light, flaky and delicious. I have experimented with pie crusts for years. The best results were achieved with a combination of two types of fats. Lard and vegan butter sticks resulted in the best flavour and texture. I have not found a vegetable shortening that is free from soy, so I use pure lard.

INGREDIENTS

1 ½ cups oat flour
½ teaspoon salt
¼ cup lard
¼ cup vegan butter
¼ cup ice cold water

Remember to choose certified gluten free oat flour

INSTRUCTIONS

1. Preheat oven to 350° F.
2. In a medium sized bowl, whisk together oat flour and salt.
3. Add cut pieces of lard and vegan butter into the flour.
4. Using two knives mix the fats into the flour until pea sized clumps form.
5. Add ice cold water, one tablespoon at a time until dough is formed.
6. Using your hands, work dough onto pie plate bottom, and up around sides, try to create an even thickness of the dough.
7. Bake for 20 minutes to achieve a partially baked pie crust. Bake for 40 minutes to achieve a fully baked pie crust.

Tip: Keeping your hands very wet with cold water will help you smooth and shape the dough. Excess water from your hands simply adds to the flaky texture.

Pumpkin Pie

The filling for this pumpkin pie is so simple and so delicious. All you need to do is blend all the ingredients together, and pour into a partially baked pie crust. What could be easier?

My Oat Flour Pie Crust compliments this pumpkin pie beautifully. For best results, partially bake the pie crust before pouring the pumpkin pie filling into the pie shell.

INGREDIENTS
1 ½ cups pumpkin puree
1 cup coconut cream*
1 cup brown sugar
1 teaspoon cinnamon
½ teaspoon nutmeg
¼ teaspoon ground cloves
3 tablespoons cornstarch

INSTRUCTIONS
1. Place all ingredients into a blender and blend until thoroughly combined. Pour pie filling into partially baked pie shell.
2. Bake pie at 350° F for 40-50 minutes. Middle should still be slightly soft; it will firm up as it cools.

Coconut cream is the thick white portion from a can of coconut milk

Lemon Meringue Pie

For best results, use the Oat Flour Pie Crust recipe. Partially bake the crust for 20minutes at 350° F; it will finish baking once the pie filling is poured in.

An egg free meringue is achieved using 'aquafaba' – whipped from chickpea brine. Sounds odd, but it works! I have included step by step instructions within this recipe. It is important to mix the brine using a stand mixer or handheld mixer for several minutes. It may seem like its not working, then suddenly the mixture begins to froth, thicken and form stiff peaks – just like egg white meringue.

LEMON FILLING INGREDIENTS

1 cup lemon juice (about 4 large lemons)
2 cups white sugar
1 teaspoon lemon zest
1 can full fat coconut milk
½ cup cornstarch
¼ teaspoon salt
1/8 teaspoon turmeric

LEMON FILLING INSTRUCTIONS

1. Add all lemon filling ingredients into a medium sauce pan, whisk to combine.
2. Place sauce pan over medium heat, whisking continually.
3. Lower heat once mixture boils, continue to whisk until mixture has thickened.
4. Remove from heat and slowly pour into partially baked oat pie crust, top with meringue.

MERINGUE INGREDIENTS

½ - ¾ cup brine from can of chickpeas
½ teaspoon cream of tartar
½ cup confectioner's (icing) sugar
½ teaspoon vanilla
½ teaspoon guar gum (optional)

MERINGUE INSTRUCTIONS

1. Pour the liquid from one can of chickpeas into a medium mixing bowl, add cream of tartar and begin mixing at medium speed.
2. Add 1 tablespoon of sugar at a time until all is incorporated, while continuously mixing.
3. Add vanilla and continue mixing until soft peaks form.
4. As an option, add guar gum until incorporated to help maintain stiff peaks.
5. Pour on top of the lemon filling, creating decorative peaks, if you wish.
6. Bake pie at 350° F for 15-20 minutes, until meringue lightly browns on top.

Key Lime Pie

A no-bake crumb crust works best for this pie. I like to use a mixture of gluten free Rice Chex and gluten free Crispix to make my crumbs. You can add the cereals to a large Ziploc bag and crush with a rolling pin, or use a food processor to make crumbs.

The pie filling needs a chance to set before it is ready to serve. It can be placed in the refrigerator for several hours or overnight. Put it in the freezer for a few hours if you want to speed up the process!

As an option, top the pie with dairy free whip cream. Check the ingredients to be sure it is safe for your allergy needs.

CRUMB CRUST INGREDIENTS
2 cups gluten free crumbs
1 tablespoon sugar
¼ cup coconut oil, melted

CRUMB CRUST INSTRUCTIONS
1. Lightly coat a pie plate with melted coconut oil, set aside.
2. Add crumbs, sugar and melted coconut oil to a medium sized mixing bowl, and stir to combine.
3. Gently press crumb mixture into prepared pie plate.
4. Place pie plate in the fridge or freezer, while preparing the pie filling, to help stabilize the crust.

KEY LIME FILLING INGREDIENTS
⅔ cup lime juice (5-6 limes)
1 teaspoon lime zest
1 can full fat coconut milk
½ cup maple syrup
1 teaspoon vanilla
⅓ cup cornstarch

KEY LIME FILLING INSTRUCTIONS
1. Add all lime filling ingredients into a medium sauce pan, whisk to combine.
2. Place sauce pan over medium heat, whisking continually.
3. Lower heat once mixture boils, continue to whisk until mixture has thickened.
4. Remove from heat and slowly pour into chilled pie crust.
5. Place entire pie into the fridge to set for several hours, or overnight.

Chocolate Cake

Rich, moist, melt in your mouth goodness. I never thought those would be words I could use to describe a Top 10 Free cake. This chocolate cake will become your new go-to for birthdays, holidays and special occasions, or any time you want to eat a simply delicious chocolate cake. No one will know it is allergy free, unless you tell them.

I have used this recipe successfully as a layer cake, cupcakes and sheet cake. It has never let me down.

WET INGREDIENTS
1 can of coconut milk
1 tablespoon apple cider vinegar
1 ¼ cups unsweetened applesauce
½ cup coconut oil (melted)
1 teaspoon vanilla extract

DRY INGREDIENTS
2 ¼ cups Gluten Free Flour Mix
1 ½ cups white sugar
1 cup cocoa powder
1 tablespoon baking powder
1 teaspoon baking soda
1 teaspoon guar gum
1 teaspoon salt

INSTRUCTIONS
1. Preheat oven to 350° F
2. Lightly brush (2) 8" round cake pans or (1) 9×13 rectangular pan with melted coconut oil. If making cupcakes, line muffin tins with cupcake liners.
3. In a medium sized mixing bowl, mix together all wet ingredients.
4. In a large sized mixing bowl, whisk together all dry ingredients.
5. Gradually add wet mixture to dry mixture. Combine until mixture is smooth
6. Slowly pour into prepared cake pans or muffin tins.
7. Bake for 30-40 minutes. Cake will be soft, but not gooey in the centre.
8. Let cool completely before frosting.

Buttercream Frosting

Dairy free buttercream frosting is simple to make. Vegan margarine is used instead of butter to give a light and fluffy texture.

There are many store bought vegan margarines available. Always read food labels to make sure it is safe for your needs. Margarine doesn't taste exactly like butter, but comes very close. Definitely better than doing without buttercream frosting!!

To make it chocolate, simply add ½ cup of cocoa powder while incorporating the icing sugar.

INGREDIENTS

1 cup vegan margarine
4 cups confectioner's (icing) sugar
2 teaspoons vanilla extract
1-2 tablespoons dairy free milk

INSTRUCTIONS

1. Add margarine and vanilla to mixing bowl and blend until smooth.
2. Gradually add sugar, while beating on low, until all the sugar is incorporated.
3. Add small amounts of milk at a time until the right consistency is reached.

Royal Icing

Enjoy decorating cookies for any occasion! Gel food colouring can be used to create infinite creative possibilities. You can spread this icing on cookies, or pipe it using icing bags and various tips. Let your creativity soar! The icing will dry and harden on the cookies, just like regular royal icing.

FROSTING INGREDIENTS
2 cups confectioners (icing) sugar
2 tablespoons water
Various gel food dyes as desired

FROSTING INSTRUCTIONS
1. Allow cookies to cool completely before frosting.
2. Add icing sugar to a medium sized bowl.
3. Add water a little bit at a time until a smooth, slightly thick consistency is reached. More water can be added to thin out if needed.
4. Add gel food dye to the icing to create any desired colour.
5. Have fun decorating!

Sugar Cookies

This sugar cookie recipe tastes like the real deal, yet is safe from the top 10 food allergens. The dough is easy to work with so you can roll it out and cut into whatever shapes you want.

COOKIE INGREDIENTS

2 ½ cups Gluten Free Flour Mix
1 teaspoon baking powder
1 tablespoon guar gum*
1 cup white sugar
½ cup vegan margarine
⅓ cup dairy free milk
1 teaspoon vanilla extract

*this is a larger than usual amount of guar gum added, yet is necessary to achieve the best results.

COOKIE INSTRUCTIONS

1. Preheat oven to 325° F; line two baking sheets with parchment paper.
2. In a large mixing bowl, cream the vegan margarine and sugar together, add vanilla extract, set aside.
3. In a separate mixing bowl, add the gluten free flour mix, baking powder and guar gum, whisk to thoroughly combine.
4. Add the dry ingredient to the margarine/ sugar mix, add dairy free milk.
5. Mix dough until all the dry ingredients are incorporated.
6. Divide the dough into two equal parts to make it easy to work with.
7. Between two sheets of parchment paper, roll dough out to ¼" thickness.
8. Cut out dough into desired shapes, transfer cookies to prepared cookie sheet, continue with the rest of dough.
9. Bake 7-11 minutes. Leave on cookie sheet for 10 minutes before transferring to cooling rack.

Shortbread Cookies

Melt in your mouth goodness is the best way to describe these cookies. I have brought them to countless gatherings over the years and they continue to be a favourite with everyone. People marvel at their soft and fluffy texture. It's always a delight to surprise people with how delicious allergy safe baking can be.

These cookies call for vegan margarine to be used instead of butter. There are many varieties of vegan margarine available. Be sure to choose one that is safe for your allergies. Try different brands until you find your favourite.

INGREDIENTS

1 cup vegan margarine
⅔ cup confectioners (icing) sugar
½ teaspoon vanilla extract
1 cup potato starch
1 cup cornstarch

INSTRUCTIONS

1. Preheat oven to 350° F.
2. Line a baking tray with parchment paper.
3. In a large mixing bowl cream vegan margarine and icing sugar, add vanilla.
4. In a separate mixing bowl whisk together cornstarch and potato starch.
5. Slowly add starches to margarine mixture and stir until everything is incorporated.
6. Drop by heaping tablespoons onto prepared baking tray.
7. Flatten cookies with a fork wet with water to keep it from sticking to cookies.
8. Bake 18-20 minutes. Allow to cool for 10 minutes before moving to a cooling rack.

Oatmeal Cookies

Oat flour alone would be too dense to use as a substitute for all gluten-free baking, but when baking cookies, oat flour is amazing! These cookies come together easily, and the dough acts much like wheat based cookie dough. The dough can be a bit sticky, so don't worry about rolling it into little balls, or too much will end up on your hands. Simply scoop the cookie dough onto a baking sheet using a tablespoon or ice cream scoop. Then, to ensure even cooking, flatten the cookies using a wet fork, this prevents the fork from sticking to the dough. Keep dipping the fork in a small bowl of water as you flatten the cookies. Once the cookies come out of the oven, let them cool on the baking tray for about 10 minutes before transferring them to a cooling rack to cool the remainder of the way. If you try to move them immediately out of the oven they can crumble. If you simply leave them for about 10 minutes, they stabilize and are ready to move or eat!

DRY INGREDIENTS
1 ½ cups gluten free oat flour
½ cup gluten free oats
½ teaspoon baking soda
½ teaspoon baking powder
¼ teaspoon guar gum

WET INGREDIENTS
¼ cup vegan margarine
½ cup maple syrup
¼ cup dairy free milk of choice
1 teaspoon vanilla extract

OPTION:
Add ½ cup allergy safe chocolate chips or raisins to the batter, stirring to combine, before scooping onto baking tray.

INSTRUCTIONS
1. Preheat oven to 350° F.
2. Line a baking tray with parchment paper.
3. In a large mixing bowl add all dry ingredients, whisk to combine, set aside.
4. In a separate medium sized mixing bowl, add all the wet ingredients, whisk to combine.
5. Add wet ingredient mixture to the dry mixture, stirring to combine.
6. Scoop a spoonful at a time onto prepared baking tray.
7. Flatten with a fork dipped in water.
8. Bake for 9-13 minutes.
9. Let cool for about 10 minutes before moving cookies from baking sheet.

About the Author

Lori Dziuba is the creator of Simply Allergy Free, a web site dedicated to helping you live with multiple food allergies.

www.SimplyAllergyFree.com

After developing multiple food allergies as an adult Lori was determined to create an abundance of recipes that are simple to prepare, safe from the Top 10 food allergens, and delicious enough for everyone to enjoy.

Email Lori with questions or comments:
info@simplyallergyfree.com

Follow her on social media:

Instagram.com/SimplyAllergyFree
Facebook.com/SimplyAllergyFree
Pinterest.ca/SimplyAllergyFree

Printed in Great Britain
by Amazon

46200222R00085